The HANGOVER HANDBOOK

DAVID OUTERBRIDGE

Illustrated by Gray Jolliffe

HARMONY BOOKS/NEW YORK

First U.S. edition 1981 by Harmony Books, a division of Crown Publishers,
Inc., One Park Avenue, New York, New York 10016. Harmony Books
is a registered trademark of Crown Publishers, Inc.
Printed in the United States of America.

Library of Congress Cataloging in Publication Data
Outerbridge, David
The Hangover Handbook

1. Hangover cures. 2. Alcohol—Physiological effect.
I. Title
TX951.096   616.86'1   81-6625   AACR2

ISBN: 0-517-545845 (cloth)
0-517-543567 (paper)

10 9 8 7 6 5 4 3 2

This book is dedicated to two most pleasurable drinking companions: T.R.M. who has the virtue of never premeditating the consequences; and R.L.H. whose predilection for cheap rum has caused us a couple of nasty biking mishaps.

In vino veritas. Before Noah, men, having only water to drink, could not find the truth. Accordingly, they became abominably wicked, and they were justly exterminated by the water they loved to drink. This good man, Noah, having seen all his contemporaries had perished by this unpleasant drink, took a dislike to it; and God, to relieve his dryness, created the vine and revealed to him the art of making *le vin*. By the aid of this liquid he unveiled more and more truth; and since this time all the best things, even the gods, have been called *divine*. He made the wine to cheer us. When you see your neighbor at table pour wine into his glass do not hasten to pour water into it. Why would you drown truth? Know that the apostle Paul advised Timothy very seriously to put wine into his water for his health; but that not one of the apostles, nor any of the holy fathers, ever watered wine.

PS In order to still more confirm you in your piety and recognition of divine providence, reflect on the position God has given the elbow. By its present location, we see it designed so that we can drink at our ease, with the glass coming just to the mouth. Let us then adore, glass in hand, that wise benevolence; let us adore and drink.

Benjamin Franklin

CONTENTS

This book has to start with a toast to Rae Lindsay. Without her long-time interest in preparing a book on the subject, *The Hangover Handbook* would never have been written. Many of the remedies, the anecdotes and the quotations have come from her research. If after reading this book you discover that life without a hangover is a pleasant way to live the least you will do is drink her health. I, myself, send champagne.

I must also thank Dr Boris Tabakoff, who devotes his professional days to the study of the effects of alcohol on the body, for his generosity in sharing some of that knowledge.

Apart from the specific contributions of others which are noted in the text, the book owes a debt to three writers who have enlightened the subject. The first is Kingsley Amis whose book *On Drink*, Jonathan Cape Ltd 1972 provides some of the better prescriptions. More than that, however, the sheer verve of his writing on the subject has helped elevate this book to a height that would otherwise not have been possible. Secondly, a word of appreciation is due to that wonderful raconteur in matters of food and drink, Waverley Root. In a long article for the *New York Times* some years back he brought together a number of important historical notes on the aftermath of drink. Finally, in a short article in *Harper's Bazaar* Kathryn Rose managed to cram dozens of useful titbits of information about coping with the ubiquitous hangover.

If you have an effective hangover cure do send it to me, care of Harmony Books, a division of Crown Publishers Inc, 1 Park Avenue, New York NY 10016.

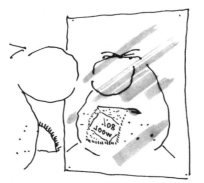

Chapter 1.

To drink and be merry

'A man hath no better thing under the sun than to eat and to drink and to be merry.'

Ecclesiastes viii, 15

Thus the Good Book advises us, and even though Ecclesiastes is annulled by others (e.g. Isaiah: 'Woe unto them that rise up early in the morning, that they may follow strong drink'), man has continued to take this advice to heart. In fact, *homo ludens* has been concocting alcoholic drinks for several million years.

During almost all of this time the alcoholic drink of man was limited to a brew he could develop by the fermentation of various plant-life: cactus (pulque), grains (beer), grapes (wine). It was not until just 1,200 years ago that the possibilities of distillation were discovered by one Jābir ibn Hayyān, an Arabic alchemist, who stumbled on to the process, the liquid of which was given the Arabic name *alkuhl*.

For almost as long there has been a continuous search for a cure for the after-affects of alcohol. However, unlike the search for the Fountain of Youth and the alchemists' dream, both of which proved illusory, there are many cures for 'the morning after'. *The Hangover Handbook* is the first comprehensive guide to the remedies for the malady known to the English-speaking peoples as a hangover. The study is long awaited. (Indeed, mere word of its existence in manuscript form has generated a flood of requests for Xeroxed copies.)

This study would be extremely morose reading if a hangover were the inevitable consequence of drink. Happily, the research has not only discovered basic ways of avoiding a hangover, but is filled with cures that produce rapid recovery should the hangover be accidentally contracted.

The Hangover Handbook will be an indispensible tool for the social drinker. My 'social drinker' is someone who drinks for the pleasures of the taste and/or effect of alcohol, usually in the company of others, but sometimes alone. It must be borne in mind, however, that alcohol is the most potent narcotic legally available without prescription, and that there are people who have passed from the point of social drinking into the disease of alcoholism. This book is not for them, nor for people whose drinking tends to produce *delirium tremens* and hallucinations.

The human race began enjoying a taste of the good stuff shortly after the Creation. It was Adam and Eve's relative, Noah, who first discovered the pleasures of a cocktail hour. Genesis reports that after the Flood receded and the Ark was grounded, 'Noah, the tiller of the soil, was the first to plant a vineyard. And he drank of the wine, and became drunk.' (And passed out, naked, in his tent.) Since that time liquor has been variously used in the consecration of sacred rites, as a medicine, as a palliative for any number of problems of mind and spirit, as an anaesthetic, as a liquid accompaniment to food, as a stimulant and as a booster for courage. In the latter role it has been so celebrated that one major English brewery calls its principal beverage Courage.

Does liquor really induce courage? Only a coward could say not. There are only four ways to create a sense of fearlessness, and a good belt of alcohol stands as the most reliable among the options. Courage used to be had from *noblesse oblige*, but ever since Karl Marx wreaked his havoc there has been less and less *noblesse*; and there was never really enough to meet the demand for *oblige* anyway. Then there is the courage of a mindless charge into a hail of bullets accompanied by the shriek *'Banzai'* (which translates into an equally mindless '10,000 years') or *'Geronimo'*, a word that gives courage to a paratrooper leaping from a plane, wondering if the parachute will open. Even the response to the more rational command, 'Come on, out of the trenches, let's give it to the Jerries', only requires that you be either (1) stupid or (2) sufficiently adroit to sublimate all natural reaction.

Least common in the non-alcoholic routes to courage is that of the occasional fanatic zealot, religious or otherwise.

Zealots eschew liquor for more complex stimulants. The *amok* of Mindinao, for example, bind their testicles tightly with rawhide. Thus crushed, the glands deliver a pain so intense that the *amok*, who has dressed in a long white smock ahead of time, races out of doors and starts killing people right, left and centre. Word will spread quickly to the constabulary which, armed with .45 calibre pistols (developed by Douglas McArthur at the turn of the century for the very purpose), will terminate the *amok*.

To conclude the point – this is not a book about courage after all; suffice it to point out that these techniques are rare compared to the use of liquor for courage-building. Said another way, more fights are started in bars than in any other environment.

Because of its magical qualities, the access to liquor has often been synonymous with power. Priests and rulers controlled the gates to the supply. Consequently the dispensation of alcohol produced a reciprocal action of servitude: allegiance. In the early 1950s the author recalls driving along the recently completed New Jersey Turnpike through the mile of great stench caused by a nearby pig farm. The owner of same was a recurring candidate for the office of President of the United States. How did he amass the necessary signatures to be placed on the ballot? By running on a platform of free beer for everyone. The move was not without precedent. In 1758 George Washington, campaigning for a seat in the legislature, had his minions hand out *three gallons* of spirits to every voter. He was elected.

Ships' captains have also had the power to dispense drink. Traditionally in the British Navy this was rum, which subsequently became Navy Grog. The latter was created when it was discovered that limes could prevent scurvy (a nasty ailment sporting bleeding gums, anaemia, etc). So the rum was cut with lime juice, and forevermore the British sailor, heretofore known as a 'tar', became a 'limey'. The etymology of 'grog' goes to the first officer to order the mixture, one Admiral Vernon, who was fond of wearing a cloak of grogram during inclement weather, and whose epithet below decks was 'Old Grog'.

Vernon deserves more than passing note as a rum cutter. He was also something of an inventor. His days aboard ship preceded the invention by Macintosh of first-class rain gear. He therefore devised his own. The grogram cape for which he was known was fine for chilly evenings but it needed modification for rainy weather. Vernon accomplished this by spreading the garment with a mixture of beeswax and pitch. This did the trick nicely. Unfortunately, the creation was not suitable for weather both wet *and* cold, as the admiral discovered one evening. Standing on the quarterdeck, he became aware that the cape had hardened into an unmovable wrapping, and in point of fact he was *unable to move*. The officer of the watch noted his predicament and had him carried below, where he soon thawed out and was again able to manoeuvre.

Capes and cocktails aside, Vernon was an interesting fellow. In the 1750s he charmed George Washington and his brother Lawrence, whom he encountered in Barbados. So impressed were the brothers with this dashing admiral that when they got back to Virginia they named the family estate after him, Mount Vernon.

For those who serve in the US Navy, ship captains hold a different kind of key – to the brig. Almost alone among the navies of the world, US warships are 'dry', and have been since Prohibition. Aboard ship there are just three things an officer must avoid doing if he wishes to become a career man. Only three, but they are taken very seriously. First, he must not embezzle from ship's stores; second, he must not mislay highly classified documents; third, he must not be caught with any alcohol. Of course the temptations attendant to the last have proved insurmountable on occasion. The most famous closet drinker was Mister Roberts who, along with his fellow conspirator the doctor, fabricated lethal potions out of the ship's medicine supplies. The most personal example for this author is the memory of the USS *Hugh Purvis*, a destroyer. In the mid 1950s as she steamed through the torrid Red Sea and the Captain sat in his air-conditioned wardroom, a select group of junior officers, having removed a quantity of vodka from the safe normally reserved for top-secret invasion plans, chilled it to proper level by hosing it with the ship's firefighting CO_2 equipment.

In addition to the potentate who held the keys to the cellar, the winemaker or brewmaster was also a man of privilege. In Wales, for example, during the Middle Ages, when the daily consumption of ale hovered around eight quarts, 'the royal brewer ranked above the court physician, and it was the King's privilege to sample privately every new cask of ale. It was further ordained that the high-ranking steward should "receive as much of every cask of plain ale as he can reach with his middle finger dipped into it, and as much of every cask of ale with spiceries as he can reach with the second joint of the middle finger".'*

---

*From *The Booze Book: The Joy of Drink*, edited by Ralph Schoenstein, Playboy Press 1974.

'O God that men should put an enemy in their mouths to steal away their brains.'

William Shakespeare

●

The effects of liquor can be various. There are people who get tipsy and find things increasingly humorous, including themselves, laughing harder and harder in their cups. For some, drink casts a rosy patina on the world about. 'Who, after wine, talks of war's hardships or of poverty?' asked Horace. Or, as Mister Dooley* says, 'There is wan thing an' on'y wan thing to be said in favor iv dhrink, an' that is that it has caused manny a lady to be loved that otherwise might've died single.' There are those who become silent, sullen, who sit and brood. There are the uglies who become pugnacious after a few drinks and challenge people to 'put up their dukes'. Whatever the mood of the drinker – and it is usually determined by the frame of mind of the person before the first drink is poured – there seems to be a general loosening of the tongue. *In vino veritas*, the Romans used to say, 'in wine, truth'. A drinker becomes relaxed and speaks with greater ease; the inhibitions lift. He may even become impelled to blurt out 'the truth', some soppy confession of wrong-doing, to the startled victim of the outrage. It is the reason that spies are always being plied with fine brandies by the enemy's attractive agentress (who also invariably hints of nymphomania). 'Drunkenness neither keeps a secret, nor observes a promise.'

There are quick and slow ways of inducing the effects of alcohol. Obviously a drink with a high percentage of alcohol will take its toll more quickly that a weak one (with some exceptions, discussed in Chapter 2). Kingsley Amis recalls: 'I once shared a half-litre bottle of Polish Plain Spirit (140° proof) with two chums. I only spoke twice, first to say, "Cut out that laughing – it can't have got to you yet," and not all that much later to say, "I think I'll go to bed now." '

Mister Dooley on Ivrything and Ivrybody by Finley Peter Dunne, Dover Publications.

Alcohol affects people in different ways:

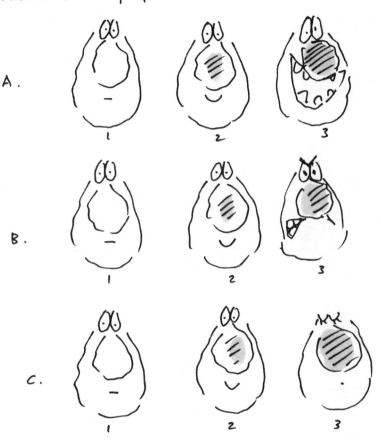

A.

1   2   3

B.

1   2   3

C.

1   2   3

Yet the drink need not be strong for early effect. An old freshman trick to get the most sensation at the minimum cost is to pour a bottle of beer into a soup-bowl and consume it by the spoonful. What happens in this case is that the slow ingestion permits complete absorption of the alcohol into the system and up into the brain, not otherwise possible. (It is said that drinking beer through a straw will produce a similar effect.)

All of this, however, borders on a discussion of just exactly what alcohol is doing to the body, which is the subject of Chapter 2.

There are many expressions in the English language for drunkenness, among them: banjaxed, besotted, bibulous, blasted, bloated, blotto, bosky, brained, canned, cherry-merry, chocked, corked, crashed, dipsy, drenched, electrocuted, foxed, flushed, fuddled, gassed, giddy, ginnified, glassy-eyed, groggy, intoxicated, jugged, juiced, lit-up, mellow, merry, muddled, newted, obfuscated, pickled, pie-eyed, pissed, primed, reeling, reely, sauced, scuppered, shattered, shit-faced, skewered, skunked, slaughtered, sloshed, swizzled, squiffed, stoned, tanked, tipsy, weltered, whacked, zonked.

More elaborate phrases for the phenomenon include: half-seas-over (nautical), flatch-kennurd (black), full of Dutch courage, in his armour, under the table, high-titty, seeing elephants, in his cups, one over the eight, and under the influence. George Lang who noted some of the above in his *Compendium of Culinary Nonsense and Trivia* adds such evocative epithets as 'has business on both sides of the way, got his little hat on, bung's his eve, got a spur in his head, got a crumb in his beard, been among the Philistines, lost his legs, got his nightcap on, got his skin full, a pinch of snuff in his wig, taken a lunar, had his wig oiled, been diddled'.

It is ironic that for all the imagery in the description for drunkenness that there is no parallel in the explication of a hangover. We speak of 'the morning after', and *Playboy* calls it 'the wrath of grapes', but there is not much more. Perhaps that is appropriate: the wonderful euphoria of the first taste, or intoxication itself, leads to hyperbole; whereas the aftermath is a time for silence.

Nonetheless the words for hangover in other languages provides some imagery. They include:

gueule de bois (French) – literally, a snout of wood;
Katzenjammer (German) – a wailing of cats;
jeg har tommermenn (Norwegian) – I have carpenters in my head
stonato (Italian) – out of tune;
and the author's favourite,
ressaca (Portuguese) – literally undertow, or line of surf, or (more figuratively) the tide has gone out.
Sonorically, of course, the Yugoslavs win with *mamurluk*.

... and, of course, 'legless'.

None of these however, really does justice to a well-rounded description of a full-blown hangover.

The head is an urn of complaints. Most immediate is a hammering headache that is both dull and intense simultaneously. To move the head causes new pains at the back of the skull, and to open the eyes sends shafts of painful light in the front. The ears ring and outside noises are unusually abrasive. The mouth is dry and feels caked. The taste is terrible and the breath feels foul (and is). The tongue and throat are parched, the chest is taut with heartburn, and any attempt to move causes severe dizziness. This sensation of queasiness immediately telegraphs itself to the stomach which is entertaining its own disorders. The dizziness compounds a feeling of general nausea; sometimes this will surge into a fit of vomiting, but more often will continue to hold the victim in a limbo of wooziness and diarrhoea, and a desire for a cathartic heave. In addition, the stomach walls have been scoured by the alcohol, producing true indigestion. The nervous system is still drugged, causing the body to experience uncontrolled shakes: this is most noticeable in the hands, but the flushes of the face and the chills of the torso are allied manifestations.

The subject of the above profile is recognized by an outsider through a number of generic features. Behind his dark glasses are a set of watery, bloodshot eyes. His breath sprays an odour of stale alcohol before him. And in between spasms he is making one of two comments: '*This* I will never do again', or 'I've got to get a cure for this before I die.'

All of this is only a cursory peep into a definition of the ailment. George Ade, in a scrap of poetry, spoke of 'a dark brown taste' – a good image, especially if it describes the morning-after of a heavy smoker. A proud drunk, the late W. C. Fields, touched on the sensitivity of the head when, following a night of over-indulgence, he complained of an Alka Seltzer fizzing in a glass of water: 'Can't anyone do something about that racket!' Fields seldom suffered from hangovers, however (see his cure, page 70), and enjoyed staying close to the magic juice. 'A woman drove me to drink,' he once explained, 'and I never even wrote to thank her.'

'Always carry a flagon of whisky in case of snake bite,' he

admonished others, 'and furthermore always carry a small snake.'

Among the organs, the mouth seems to be the most usual object of complaint, albeit the least important, after a night of drinking. A furry mouth, a scummy mouth, a tongue with whiskers, a bird-cage mouth, itchy teeth, and 'my mouth feels like the ——— (ethnic, optional) army walked through barefoot.' Obviously this malady can be remedied by a quick rinse with highly flavoured detergent manufactured for the purpose.

On a more fundamental level there are three ways to overcome a hangover: we can endure it, numb it, or eliminate it. Let us briefly examine these alternatives.

Endure it This is the stoic approach. It is also, unfortunately, the only guaranteed approach according to a number of doctors, drinkers, columnists and overly righteous folk. The doctors (who are usually specialists in dermatology or podiatry, and have long since forgotten their pre-med chemistry primers) invoke medical mumbojumbo as follows: poison has been ingested and must be evacuated before a poison-free environment is restored. Nonsense! And columnists (who know better in their private lives) can churn out more pungent copy at holiday time if they embellish the miseries of overindulgence. Nonsense! Drinkers who never knew better (and it was not easy before the appearance of this book) just assumed it was a necessary penance. 'If you want to dance you have to pay the fiddler,' an officer of the late USS *Hugh Purvis* would intone upon relieving the watch after leaving port. Apart from inevitability, this counsel also carried a sense of superior knowledge — i.e. *you* are suffering more than *me* – but could be discounted upon the observation that the speaker was, himself, wearing dark sunglasses in the almost totally dark radar room.

Numb it Prescription drugs and over-the-counter pops such as paracetamol will erase a headache and related pain. But this is a passive solution and leaves other elements of the hangover in place. It is also a dangerous entry into drug use.

Eliminate it This philosophy banners the mood and substance of this book. Once you understand the psychodynamics of your body's encounter with alcohol (Chapter 2) you will be able to measure your condition and deal with it effectively from the panoply of cures presented.

Essentially there are three points within a session of projected drinking at which an individual may start working to eliminate what could become, or is, a hangover: before, during and after. *Before* is represented only briefly in the recipe section because many of the suggestions are beyond the control of the average citizen, e.g. to be six foot eight and weigh 270 pounds (big bodies fare better). *During*, likewise, is not widely represented. After all, who wants to start a programme of preventive maintenance as they sit among friends in a cosy bar enjoying a few drinks? And late at night, falling into bed, the precaution may be forgotten.

After This is where the research has unearthed a gold mine. There are the internal remedies – herbal, medicinal, nutritional, restorative. The book exposes false cures, and steps gingerly into the matter of placebos. (A placebo is a non-functional prescription that becomes functional because the user thinks it is functional.) Marty Ingels, a Hollywood comedian of some note, describes the ultimate placebo in connection with alcohol, albeit not hangovers. He writes:

The mere *mention* of 'drink' only brings to mind a most incredible period of my life after having landed in Hollywood at age twenty-two and almost immediately signing for a network TV series ... I suddenly found myself unable to go to work – unable to *get out of bed* – without first, a drink, then a *few*, and finally, a screwdriver *thermos* that stayed with me till the last shot of the last hour of the day. But only one day stands out in my memory...

It was the day of my big scene – and so the morning began with my filling my courage-thermos extra high with vodka and orange juice – and, as the day progressed and my responsibility increased, my 'sips' got bigger and more frequent till the giant thermos was empty and I was totally bombed, performing my crucial scenes with an unusually high dose of my borrowed courage.

Finally the day was over ... Staggering delicately into the house, I met my wide-eyed wife with a giant burst of tears, tripping some and bemoaning my woesome fate as the 'first Jewish drunk in America'.

'What the hell are you smiling about?' I screeched to a halt.

'Nothing,' she said. 'Gowan with your story. You said it was the booze that brought you through the day?'

'You're damn right. It was the first time I emptied my screwdriver thermos to the last – and look at me – I'm whacked, I'm finished.'

'You're finished, huh?'

'Yes.'

'You're sure.'

'Yes, dammit, I'm sure.'

'Well,' she shook her head like a lab technician, 'maybe not.'

'What the hell do you mean?'

'Well,' her tight lips giving way to a cautious smile, 'this morning when you were filling your thermos with the orange juice and vodka, I waited till you were shaving ... and then poured it all out and filled it again with only orange juice!'

Finally, the remedy section includes the external cures (saunas, flagellation, and the like).

Thus this book moves through all the ramifications of a hangover and its cure. What a happy event! For what ailment, more than any other, has been the enduring burden of man, if not the hangover? Across cultures and through time it has been cursed, denied, exaggerated and even *celebrated*. This last phenomenon is to be found among the Dayak of Borneo. These sage people believe the hangover to be a sacred moment; and to induce the quintessential affliction on certain occasions, proceed to become stinking drunk. The following day in the throes of a monumental hangover they are able to see into the future, to foretell events, And so they sit in their jungle clearings hungover and oracular.

At this moment in more mundane circumstances than among the Dayak, on every continent tens of thousand of people are trudging to work nursing throbbing heads, cursing queasy stomachs, doctoring furry mouths with peppermints, muttering such thoughts as 'I'd have to feel better to die.' Many are eyeing the clock, calculating the time until lunch and the first taste of Guinness or a crisp Martini to take the edge off the misery.

There is a certain fraternal spirit among hangover victims. Conventioneers, holidaymakers, even serious hunters and other early risers enjoy a rolling of eyes as they greet each other in the morning. They feast on the descriptions they fashion for each other about just how awful they feel. In some perverse way, pleasure is derived from revealing the most detailed anatomical revelations of the personal hangover. And everyone is convinced that his own malaise is many times worse than anyone else's.

Now this ancient scourge that is the human lot is to come to an end.

FIRST INTERLUDE

The Rabbit

Valnikov slept in the yellow rubber raincoat. He slept crossways on the daybed, one shoe on, one shoe off. He slept on his back, head tilted, face florid. His eyes were almost stuck shut from sour vomitus belches. Valnikov snored and wheezed, and as usual, dreamed of the rabbit. He cried out in his sleep and awoke when the hunter cut the rabbit's throat, broke the rabbit's jaws, and began peeling the skin back over the rabbit's face. The tearing muscle hissed and jawbones crackled in the powerful hands.

'Lord God!' he sobbed and awoke himself.

It was hard to tell where he hurt most. His head felt like a huge festering sponge. His back felt hinged. If he tried to straighten, the crusted rusty hinges would scream.

He almost screamed when he stood. Now at least he knew what hurt most: the festering sponge. His head was mushy. Lord God, have mercy. He fell back on the bed, moaning. Then Misha said, *'Gavno.'*

'Please, Misha,' Valnikov pleaded. 'Oh, my head!'

But Misha repeated, *'Gavno, gavno, gavno.'*

Misha only knew one Russian word and it meant *shit*. In fact, it was the only *human* word he could say.

Valnikov glared with one blazing eye and saw that Misha was standing on Grisha's head. Misha twittered and chirped and sang for his master, who held his ears and cried: 'Please, Misha, please. Noise *hurts*.'

But Misha just tossed his lovely emerald head, preened, and said: *'Gavno.'*

Shit.

Then Valkinov became aware that he was soaked by the perspiration from the oppressive rubber raincoat, and by the dream of the rabbit, which always brought night sweats.

Misha yelled: *'Gavno!'* like a challenge and through the agonizing mist of the vodka hangover Valnikov was amazed to see that Misha had just crapped on Grisha's head. As though he truly understood what the word meant! Well maybe he did. Who could say what a bird or a man understood.

It wasn't the shit, it was the noisy *'gavno'* which angered Grisha. The little rodent lunged at Misha, who squawked and flew to the trapeze at the top of the seven-foot cage. The furious little animal then sulked around the floor of the enormous cage until he found a comfortable place to settle down again. His head was covered with *gavno*.

The furnished bachelor apartment on Franklin Avenue was crisscrossed with clothesline which ran from the top of the giant animal cage to a nail pounded over the bathroom door frame. Three pairs of underwear and two pairs of socks were hung on that indoor clothesline, thanks to the endless queue of women at the apartment building's coin-operated clothes dryer.

There were unwashed glasses and dishes and empty vodka bottles on the formica table, on the plastic chairs, on the kitchen sink, in the kitchen sink. Stacked higher than the dishes and glasses was a vast collection of recordings, in and out of album covers. The records were on the kitchen table, on the chairs, on the sink. And two were *in* the sink – which puzzled him this morning. At least they weren't damaged by water since he only washed dishes one at a time when necessary.

The tiny cluttered apartment boasted one great luxury, aside from the large record collection: a Micro Seike turntable and two Epicure speakers worth a thousand dollars each, capable of making the whole apartment house thump and vibrate.

Valnikov stood, stripped off the rubber raincoat and all of his wet outer clothing. He forced himself to march to the bathroom and showered in icy water, unaware for the moment that he had forgotten to remove his underwear and one sock.

His broad red face was bleeding in three places after he shaved. He spilled tea on his blue necktie when he drank, unable to hold the shaking glass of tea with both hands. Then he put the gerbil's food in Misha's dish and the parakeet's food in Grisha's dish. He was halfway out of the door before he thought that he had possibly made a mistake. He returned and saw that he had.

He groaned, and shooed Misha away from the rodent's dish.

'Please, Misha, eat your own food.'

His voice thundered in his ears, through the flaming mush of his brain, through the infected tissue.

'Oh, never mind,' he said. 'Go ahead and eat Grisha's food. Grisha, you eat Misha's food today.'

He hobbled towards the door again, looking at his watch, listing from side to side. Then he realized that a burrowing rodent from southern Russia could never jump high enough to eat a parakeet's food in a feeding tray five feet above his head.

Valnikov managed to switch the food. Corn and barley for the gerbil, gravel and seed for the parakeet. Then he gave the little creatures water and looked at them.

'Are you two even slightly appreciative,' he moaned, 'of the pain this is giving me?'

Misha answered him. The parakeet had been swinging on his trapeze, his back to Valnikov. The emerald bird did a deliberate forward fall, gripping the tiny bar in his claws. When he was hanging upside down, staring directly into Valnikov's wet fiery eyes, Misha said: *'Gavno.'*

From *The Black Marble* by Joseph Wambaugh. Weidenfeld & Nicolson, 1978; Futura, 1978.

Chapter 2.

The logic of a hangover remedy

*'Quemadmodum inter tortores habitare
nolim, sic ne inter popinas quidem.'**

In order to understand the logic of a hangover remedy, and
to be able intelligently to create your own, it is necessary first
to have a clear picture of what alcohol is doing to the body.

Alcohol is a mild anaesthetic, among other things. Once it
arrives in the stomach it begins to be picked up by the
bloodstream, which carries it to the brain. The first sensations upon its arrival there are of a 'high', a lightening of
the head, a state of euphoria. The average body can absorb
and metabolize approximately one ounce of 80° proof liquor
an hour. If this intake is not greatly exceeded, the euphoria
will continue. However, if this amount is significantly
exceeded (e.g. 3 oz) the brain begins to be more severely
affected, causing a disruption of motor faculties. More, and
speech becomes slurred, muscle control is lessened; more,
and a stupor follows, then a coma. At this point the alcohol is
acting as ether would. It is for this reason that old-time
doctors kept a good supply of the stuff in their baggage.
When necessary, it was poured down a patient's throat
before the amputation of a leg, or other serious surgery.

The big difference between alcohol and ether, of course, is
speed – which is why, on occasion, doctors have preferred the
latter for home use as well. In the nineteenth century, for
example, the use of ether among physicians in England was
quite popular.

Exactly what happens upon the arrival of the liquor in the
brain is a matter of some current dispute. One school of
thought among the professionals who have studied the

---

*The gist of which is, I avoid bars like the plague.

phenomenon is that alcohol numbs the inhibitor cells (the disinhibitory theory). A more current hypothesis is that alcohol acts as an excitory agent on certain of the brain cells. However, the argument has no relevance for conduct during an evening of drinking. What is important to remember is that the neurons (nerve cells) are being attacked on their membranes by the alcohol and are being forced to adapt.

The degree to which an individual experiences euphoria from drink, and how quickly, is dependent on his particular make-up. Over a period of time the inherent sensitivity of a person who drinks changes – a tolerance is developed, similar to the calluses created on the hands of someone who uses them for manual work. This is why a first-time drinker will get 'high' on less than a seasoned one. Sensitivity is also determined to some degree by one's genetics. Laboratory experiments with mice have borne this out. Two groups of mice, otherwise similar, were bred: one for sensitivity to alcohol, the other for resistance to alcohol. Both groups were given the same quantity of alcohol. The latter group were quite unaffected, while the former were literally knocked on their backs – feet in the air.

Finally, in addition to the sensitivity of brain cells, the mass of one's body helps determine how quickly and to what extent a drink is going to affect a person – the larger the person, the more buffering the system can provide against the effect of liquor. (See the table on page 34 to appreciate exactly how much variation does exist in the effect of liquor in people of different sizes.)

Ideally, then, a partygoer or business-function attendee drinks only enough to reach the pleasurable state of euphoria, with inhibitions relaxed and a cheery outlook on surrounding events. Unfortunately, one often drinks far more than this amount without perhaps even meaning to, and becomes drunk. Contrary to a popular fear, this does not result in the automatic death of legions of brain cells. A few may succumb – ones already on the list, so to speak – but the toll is not massive. However, the other after-effects of too much alcohol are the concern of this book. It is time, therefore, to examine these in order to be prepared with the necessary knowledge for eliminating the unpleasantnesses attached thereto.

The ingestion of alcohol produces four basic effects that it is important for the drinker to understand:

1 Transformation This is the sequence of events that take place in the body machinery once some alcohol is consumed.

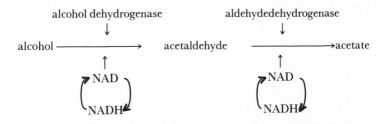

After alcohol has entered the liver, an enzyme called alcohol dehydrogenase begins to transform it into a new substance: acetaldehyde. This is a bad substance, much more poisonous than alcohol. If it is not further converted by the liver it will be released into the bloodstream. From there it will be conveyed to the brain, the adrenals and other points, causing disphoria, stress, nausea and other unpleasant effects. (In certain treatment programmes alcoholics are given a pill, Antabuse, that blocks the metabolism of acetaldehyde in the liver. If the subject then drinks alcohol acetaldehyde will accumulate and the body will rebel violently with chills, vomiting, etc. This consequence is so pronounced that the alcoholic will normally forgo drinking as long as he is on the pill.)

For the normal drinker the liver, upon creating the acetaldehyde, will employ a second enzyme to make the secondary transformation to acetate, a relatively benign substance. This entire sequence, alcohol to acetaldehyde to acetate, moves along with more or less efficiency depending on the quantity of alcohol consumed and the degree to which the body is prepared to deal with it. (For certain particular populations there is an additional difficulty. The Japanese, for example, are genetically weak in the necessary enzymes to complete the sequence. This means that they are less able to tolerate alcohol. That fact, in turn, has developed into a cultural phenomenon, the specialized way of ritualistic drinking from tiny cups. Liquor is taken, but in small amounts over a lengthy period of time.)

While the enzymes in the illustration, alcohol dehydrogenase and aldehydedehydrogenase, are active, a second co-factor must also be introduced into the metabolic process. This is a nicotonic acid derivative (NAD). NAD contributes to the metabolism (burning away) of both alcohol and the acetaldehyde. As it does so, however, the NAD is itself transformed into something else: NADH. To continue to metabolize ethanol the liver must reconvert the NADH back to NAD.

Should these two processes occur most efficiently – the ones illustrated below the sequence of alcohol to acetate – the body should be free of many of the unpleasant after-effects of alcohol, known collectively as a hangover; and will be, with some exceptions which must also be prepared for and conquered.

Allied to the process just described is one such factor. If the liquor we drank was a pure laboratory-grade ethyl alcohol (diluted with water, perhaps) what is described above would be all the activity the liver had to concern itself with. Unfortunately, what we usually take for an evening or luncheon series of drinks is quite impure. Whether distilled or simply fermented, the liquid contains a number of disruptive chemicals. Some of these come from the types of yeast and sugar used in the fabrication. The rest are products of the flavouring and colouring process. These elements are called *congeners*. They may include fusel oils (a sometimes varnish ingredient), organic acids, even aldehydes (similar to the middle product in the illustration that the body is trying so hard to eliminate). Some of these substances are so toxic that if taken straight they would be lethal. To avoid the congeners as much as possible, a person should drink the versions of alcohol closest to the pure version, i.e. take white wine instead of red, drink vodka instead of bourbon. Congeners that are taken into the body's system along with the alcohol have to be metabolized or eliminated along with the alcohol and its by-products before a healthy and well-feeling entity is restored.

Following this description, a number of alternative cures

become important. First, one should try to keep the rate of alcohol release into the body nearly equal with its ability to complete the metabolism of alcohol–acetaldehyde–acetate. This can be helped beforehand by eating proper foods. A fatty or oily food will line the stomach and duodenum walls to inhibit a too-rapid rate of absorption; proteins will aid the body processes; and starches will absorb alcohol in the stomach and moderate their delivery to the bloodstream and body tissues.

Second, if the liquor we are consuming contains congeners such as aldehyde, we want to be rid of them. Here there are two choices. The more preferable is to gather and absorb the acetaldehyde before it reaches the bloodstream (this is also true of the acetaldehyde or acetate when it is produced). Charcoal has this ability: it is an absorbent. Less known to the average drinker, but performing a similar job on the system, is a chelator: cabbage. A chelator is a substance that binds elements together with itself and takes them away. (Note the re-occurring use of cabbage as a remedy for hangover throughout history.) Vitamin C is also a chelating agent.

The second, and less preferable, choice is to metabolize the poisons; less preferable because it is less efficient. Here one must be aware of the difficulty the NAD–NADH–NAD cycle is having completing itself and in turn being useful to the metabolism process. Fructose (plentiful in honey) and oxygen are good boosters for the NAD cycle.

Probably some combination of absorption and bolstering metabolism will be present in most of the effective remedy menus a reader will devise.

2 *Altered brain cells* As was discussed earlier, alcohol can affect the neurons to produce a state of euphoria, and beyond that to anaesthetize the cells. The body, being a wonderful instrument of symmetry, can adapt and compensate for this intrusion. Just as the skin and vital organs adapt themselves to protect from a sudden exposure to cold, so do the brain cells cope with a depressant. The way they do this is to protect themselves by changing the cell walls to compensate for the depressant. The result? After the alcohol has gone from the brain, cells which have adapted by becoming more sensitive remain in this adapted state for a time. The alcohol adapted state is not conducive to normal function. Thus we experience hypersensitivity, hyper-excitability. It is the reason that sound and light seem more extreme on the morning after, and why W. C. Fields complained of the jarring noise of an Alka Seltzer tablet fizzing.

The cure for this phenomenon is surprisingly simple: allow the brain cells to make a *gradual* return to their normal, non-alcoholic-reactive state. Enter the hair of the dog. A small quantity of alcohol will allow the cells to ease their way back to normal without the abrupt, disquieting shock. This matter of physiology is likewise the basis of the bitters remedies. Bitters are a blend of tinctures of herbs, and a tincture is an alcoholic extract of the substance. Most bitters are, in fact, as strong as vodka or whisky.

3 *Replenishment* Alcohol is a dehydrator, pulling moisture from the body. It is also a diuretic, causing the body to evacuate liquid in the form of urine. Alcohol causes important elements such as magnesium to depart from their normal levels in the blood into inaccessible storage areas. Also hidden in this way are calcium (proving that the Assyrians were instinctively correct to prescribe crushed swallows' beaks for a hangover) and potassium (a lack of which can cause tremors, but which is plentiful in oranges and tomatoes). Alcohol washes away vitamins B_1, B_6 and C. The proper armament, therefore, will be to keep the body stocked up with these elements before, during and after a drinking session; and if this is forgotten *en passage*, then certainly the next morning. (This is the reason why beer and allied drinks are a healthy antidote to the hangover: they are vitamin rich.)

4 REM Each night after you go to bed you are normally giving part of your sleep to dreaming sleep, or as scientists call it, rapid-eye-movement (REM) sleep. This form, which occurs four or five times a night, each for a period of twenty to thirty minutes, is important. Studies have been conducted that show that if a person is awakened every time he is moving into REM sleep, and thus deprived of dreaming sleep, after three days he is transformed into a raving psychotic. (REM is named for the observable movement of the eyes under the closed lids following the events of a story that is being dreamed.)

For reasons not yet fully understood, alcohol inhibits REM sleep. It is why, nonetheless, a person will go to bed drunk – anaesthetized – yet wake up early, be unable to sleep and be tired and irritable the next day. In extreme encounters with alcohol 'REM rebound' can occur after a person has stopped drinking for some time. Denied REM sleep, the system copes by producing dreams in the midst of waking hours, the well-known hallucinations of pink elephants and other fantasies. The prevention of REM loss is dependent on temperance and ensuring that the body is equipped to absorb and metabolize alcohol efficiently.

Shibboleths Almost any remedy can be understood from these observations. For example, rolling naked in the snow is one

31

way to excite the blood pumping through the system and increase the inhalation of oxygen, both of which lead to the metabolism of alcohol, acetaldehydes and acetate; the splendours of coitus will do the same (see page 92 for Kingsley Amis on the subject). On the other hand, some false cures will be identified. A painkiller for a headache will not cure the inequity, only hide it: liver extracts are not going to rebuild a damaged organ, but will deliver a store of vitamins; spicy foods are not going to do more than tidy up the mouth. Yet some of the old-fashioned cures like bicarbonate of soda are, by their definition, an equalizer for acetate (an acid that is balanced in the blood by the bicarbonate of soda).

Take your drinking seriously. You are ingesting a substance that is disruptive to your body, and elements of which are truly poisonous. Prepare for it, enjoy it, but then clean up and restore your wonderful system.

A hangover is a scream of pain – and alert – from your system. You now know that a hangover is a composition of four basic maladies, all of which can be attended to:

1 the presence of toxins
2 maladapted neurons
3 loss of necessary minerals and vitamins
4 loss of REM sleep

The cure for the first is to eliminate the toxins either by trapping or by metabolizing. For the second, bring the cells back to their normal state of an alcohol-free experience *slowly* through the judicious use of alcohol as buffer.

For the third, replenish. Lastly, prepare the system for maximum and efficient metabolism through temperate use of alcohol, and arrange generous sleep time for the following night.

The following tables are provided as a guide for estimating what effect the drinks you are planning to take are going to have upon your system. This information assumes that you are average: that you are not meeting Bacchus for the first time; nor Japanese.

Table 1

Consumption per hour of ounces of 80° proof or its equivalent	percentage of alcohol in the blood	probable consequences
1	.05 or less	relaxing, no after-effect
2	.08 – .1	inhibitions less, carefree
3	.1 – .2	muscle and speech control affected
5	.2 – .4	staggering, incoherent (very drunk confused, stuporous)
8 or more	.4 or more	unconscious (equivalent of surgical anaesthesia) anaesthesia of breath and heart controls in danger of death

Don't laugh, but my head feels like a balloon!

For those on a diet (most of us), the table below shows the more weight you lose the less able to cope with alcohol you are.

Table 2*

body weight in lb	1½ oz drinks of 80° proof, or equivalent taken during an evening of drinking, and percentages of alcohol in the blood							
	1	**2**	**3**	**4**	**5**	**6**	**7**	**8**
100	.038	.075	.113	.150	.188	.225	.263	.300
120	.031	.063	.094	.125	.156	.188	.219	.250
140	.027	.054	.080	.107	.134	.161	.188	.214
160	.023	.047	.070	.094	.117	.141	.164	.188
180	.021	.042	.063	.083	.104	.125	.146	.167
200	.019	.038	.056	.075	.094	.113	.131	.150
220	.017	.034	.051	.068	.085	.102	.119	.136
240	.016	.031	.047	.063	.078	.094	.109	.125

*Based on figures computed by the New Jersey Division of Motor Vehicles.

SECOND INTERLUDE

I was slumped on my bed in the Flamingo, feeling dangerously out of phase with my surroundings. Something ugly was about to happen. I was sure of it. The room looked like the site of some disastrous zoological experiment involving whiskey and gorillas. The ten-foot mirror was shattered, but still hanging together – bad evidence of that afternoon when my attorney ran amok with the coconut hammer, smashing the mirror and all the light-bulbs.

We'd replaced the lights with a package of red and blue Christmas tree lights from Safeway, but there was no hope of replacing the mirror. My attorney's bed looked like a burned-out rat's nest. Fire had consumed the top half, and the rest was a mass of wire and charred stuffing. Luckily, the maids hadn't come near the room since that awful confrontation on Tuesday.

I had been asleep when the maid came in that morning. We'd forgotten to hang out the 'Do Not Disturb' sign ... so she wandered into the room and startled my attorney, who was kneeling, stark naked, in the closet, vomiting into his shoes ... thinking he was actually in the bathroom, and then suddenly looking up to see a woman with a face like Mickey Rooney staring down at him, unable to speak, trembling with fear and confusion.

'She was holding that mop like an axe-handle,' he said later. 'So I came out of the closet in a kind of running crouch, still vomiting, and hit her right at the knees ... it was pure instinct; I thought she was ready to kill me ...

and then, when she screamed, that's when I put the icebag on her mouth.'

Yes, I remembered that scream ... one of the most terrifying sounds I'd ever heard. I woke up and saw my attorney grappling desperately on the floor right next to my bed with what appeared to be an *old woman*. The room was full of powerful electric noise. The TV set, hissing at top volume on a nonexistent channel. I could barely hear the woman's muffled cries as she struggled to get the icebag away from her face ... but she was no match for my attorney's naked bulk, and he finally managed to pin her in a corner behind the TV set, clamping his hands on her throat while she babbled pitifully: 'Please ... please ... I'm only the maid, I didn't mean nothin' ...'

From *Fear and Loathing in Las Vegas* by Hunter S. Thompson, Paladin, 1972

Chapter 3

A perfect evening of heavy drinking and no hangover

There are an infinite number of ways to combine the variety of coony tactics contained in these pages to remain hangover-free in spite of an extremely lengthy bout of drinking. What follows is one man's route through the maze of choices of antidotes before, during and after imbibing the alcohol.

6.00 p.m. You and your girl friend sit down for a cocktail. For this evening you have chilled a fifth of vodka in the freezer. (Vodka is free of congeners, and cold drinks work slower.) From the ice box you remove a pound of fresh Beluga caviar (very high in protein). For an hour you feast on the little eggs, chased down with shots of vodka which you serve in little glasses, drunk neat. Shortly after seven o'clock both the vodka and caviar containers are empty. You are feeling happy – euphoric – awash in the pleasing sensations that a gorging on caviar can produce.

7.30 p.m. Dinnertime. You have prepared the delicious speciality of Nîmes, *brandade de morue* (rich in olive oil, milk and fish). You share a wonderful Mersault with this; and after a salad, conclude the meal with a bowl of freshly cut orange salad flavoured with kirsch.

8.30 p.m. Time to go out. You head for a local drinking place, where you meet some friends. You decide to have a cognac; 'sort of put a cap on the dinner', you explain. Then you switch to Laphroaig, a smoky single-malt scotch from Islay. You spend the rest of the evening drinking this. Upon returning home you each have a bottle of India Pale Ale to slake a final thirst. Then just before getting into bed you drink two glasses of water and take two aspirins, vitamins A, B1, B6, C and D, a pill each of calcium, magnesium and potassium.

During the evening you have drunk:

> a ½ bottle of vodka
> a ½ bottle of wine
> a snifter of cognac
> 8 scotches
> a bottle of ale

– enough for a considerable hangover.

6.30 a.m. You awaken and reach for the oxygen canister on the bedside table and take eight deep snorts, then return to sleep.

7.30 a.m. You awaken and reach for your girl friend and execute the Kingsley Amis cure (see page 92), then return to sleep.

9.00 a.m. You awaken and enjoy a breakfast of two grapefruit halves slathered in honey, a slice of calf's liver with bacon.

9.30 a.m. At this point you should feel absolutely A1, but if you think you are only A2, take either a Fernet Branca or one hair of the dog (choice optional).

Chapter 4

Remedies

The remedies that follow have been coded with a key that will help distinguish the more effective ones from those that merely pose as cures. While in the evaluation of remedies, I and my cohorts have tried to be accurate in these matters, readers may wish to modify the coding with their own results. As explained in the chapter on physical effects of alcohol, different people react differently to alcohol, so it should come as no surprise that they will react differently to the cures as well.

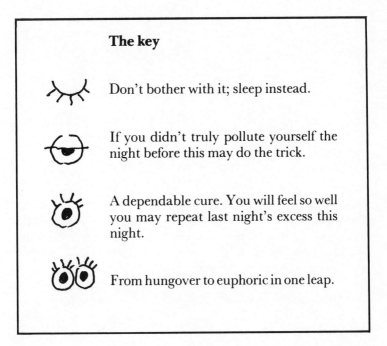

The key

Don't bother with it; sleep instead.

If you didn't truly pollute yourself the night before this may do the trick.

A dependable cure. You will feel so well you may repeat last night's excess this night.

From hungover to euphoric in one leap.

BEFORE AND DURING A NIGHT OF DRINKING

William F. Buckley Jr
'Don't drink the night before.'

If you read about the ways to prevent the rapid absorption of alcohol in Chapter 2 you will have noted that the authorities on the subject recommend, among other things, eating protein, drinking milk and ingesting some fatty or oily substances. ('Drink a beaker of olive oil' is the crass suggestion of some.) The following dish is a favourite lunch in Provence and the Languedoc of France. It was not invented for purposes of preventive medicine, but rather as a rich and subtle use of salt cod – for centuries a staple of the diet from Italy to Norway. Yet, miraculously, *brandade de morue* contains the three most effective agents in the alcohol-tempering scale.

Brandade de morue

2 lb salt cod
2 cloves garlic
1 cup milk
1 cup olive oil
pepper

Soak the cod in cold water for at least twelve hours, changing the water a couple of times. Place in a saucepan of cold water and gently bring to the boil. Immediately remove from the water. Flake the meat, discarding any bones. Heat the milk and oil in separate saucepans. Place the cod and garlic in a mortar and mash into a paste. Then bit by bit alternately add the milk and oil, mashing all the time. The final mixture will be a silky, pale yellow affair, the consistency of mashed potatoes. Serve lukewarm with slices of unbuttered toast.

Following the logic in Chapter 2 as far as keeping the blood-stream moving along to get that alcohol vented from the organs, this next remedy makes sense. Tangos are especially appropriate – movement without frenzy.

Dancing*

In between drinks. If alone, be sure to put your drink down while you dance, or the exercise will not produce the desired results.

One can tell by the very vibes that come off this remedy that it is chock full of goodness. It has, however, its complications. Taken by the spoonful, straight, peanut butter has been known to lodge in the throat and kill a person by asphyxiation. On the other hand, trying to mix the milk with it, instead of using the milk as a chaser, might be a most difficult enterprise. One variation suggested by the inventor of the remedy is to take two slices of bread and slather them with mayonnaise, then spread the peanut butter on *this*, which acts as a primitive launching lubricant to the stomach.

---

*Because it is often impossible to tell if a couple are dancing for the pleasure of it or as an anti-hangover precaution, it is best never to cut in during a dance if the premises are serving drinks as well as music.

Richard Saltonstall Jr

2 tablespoonfuls of chunky peanut butter
a tall glass of milk

Taken just before going to bed.

MEDICINAL

Vitamins are contained in many of the remedies in this book. In fact, the restorative power of these concoctions is often solely attributable to a vitamin-rich ingredient, e.g. orange juice or Tantamiento de Choque. Other remedies work partly because they contain a hair of the dog and partly due to their vitamin package, e.g. a Bloody Mary among the compound recipes and beer among the single-item remedies.

The main advantage of taking vitamins in pill form is that it is quick – especially important if they are being taken during the final moment before crashing into bed. The disadvantage, obviously, is that there is no fun involved (compared to Gail's Giggle, for example, see page 49).

If you are electing the pill alternative, here is a good mix of vitamins as an alcohol purge. However, check with your doctor to be sure you do not have an unusual vitamin imbalance.

Vitamins

A – 2 × normal daily dosage
B₁ – 4 × normal daily dosage
B₆ – 4 × normal daily dosage
C – 500–1000 mg
Nioxim – 10–20 mg
calcium – 250 mg
magnesium – 250 mg
potassium – 1 teaspoon of potassium chloride solution

Antacids are useful for only one aspect of a hangover – gastric distress. If the head feels all right, and other normal symptoms of a hangover are absent, but the stomach is in a tumult, by all means take one of the pills – Rolaids, etc – that are always being hawked in advertisements. It should settle things.

Antacids

*One or two pills of your favourite brand
or as directed on the package.*

Aspirin works in the opposite way to antacids. It will help cure a headache but will irritate the stomach lining and make things worse in the nether regions. If you think an aspirin is called for you are better advised to take an aspirin substitute.

Aspirin

*Two pills of an aspirin substitute,
or as directed on the package.*

A number of chemists devise their own remedies, which they market to a faithful clientele. Some keep their ingredients a big secret, while others dutifully note what is inside the bottle. The mix of D. R. Harris & Co. of St James's St, London, is instructive for an understanding of the genre. It contains a series of tinctures, which means that it is highly alcoholic. There is a little camphor, which gives a mothball freshness to the olfactory senses. And it contains some chloroform for good measure. As the chemist claims, 'This celebrated preparation has, for over a century, enjoyed a great reputation as a rapid restorative.'

A Chemist's Pick-me-up

Available from D. R. Harris & Co. (By Appointment to HM Queen Elizabeth The Queen Mother, Chemists) and other chemists around the globe. Administer according to the dosages indicated.

A number of specialists suggest going out-of-doors and taking deep breaths of fresh air. The theory is that the process of metabolism will be accelerated by the extra oxygen.

The author can attest to the truth of this. In the mid 1950s he was briefly stationed at a naval air station where drinks at the officers' club cost ten cents. As a result (knowing a bargain when we saw one) reveille could have had, each morning, the implication of Taps. Fortunately, Uncle Sam's pilots knew what to do. Down to a waiting line of jet aircraft they would lead us, turn on the oxygen masks, everyone would suck away on the good stuff, and lo and behold we would be recovered.

Oxygen

Twenty minutes of normal air breathed deeply in a pollution-free environment
or
several deep breaths of pure O2
from a jet aircraft or a home canister.

For centuries charcoal has been taken internally to help detoxify the contents of the stomach. Charcoal is a good cleansing agent, which is one reason why things such as liquor are filtered through it before going into the bottle. Thus it is not surprising that some wag decided that it could absorb the foul residues of over-drinking. Chemists are mixed in their opinion about this credo, but nonetheless continue to sell great quantities annually of the black gritty tablets. (NB What you buy in a drugstore is what you should take if charcoal is for you. The briquettes you buy for barbeque are not for munching.)

Charcoal

Four to six tablets, or more as directed on the container.

Although the label advertises itself as a 'bitter stimulant to the appetite', Fernet Branca is known the world over as a cure for hangovers.

I first encountered the product aboard a British man-of-war, where the wardroom maintained a full bar for the pleasures of the officers. Yet these gentlemen had to be in tiptop condition come the time to stand watch or go into battle. How did they avoid the morning-after syndrome? Fernet Branca.

Fernet Branca is made of the extracts of aloes, gentian, zedoary, cinchona, calumba, galangal, rhubarb, bryonia, angelica, myrrh, camomile, saffron and peppermint oil. A veritable Culpepper with, it should be noted, an alcoholic proof of almost 80°. (This fact makes it extremely difficult to determine whether the remedy belongs in the medicinal section or under 'hair of the dog'.)

Because of the ingredients, the first time Fernet Branca is experienced the taster may gag, in which case it is best just to belt the black liquid down. Over time, however, a person can come to enjoy the bitter aromatic taste and may wind up sipping the drink as an aperitif.

Fernet Branca
1 or 2 oz taken neat

For those who become enamoured of the flavour of Fernet Branca and who wish to extend its bouquet to a longer drink, there is the Sputnik.

Sputnik
1 oz Fernet Branca
2 oz vodka
1 teaspoonful fresh lemon or lime juice
$^1/_2$ teaspoonful sugar
ice cubes

Combine the Fernet Branca, vodka and sugar and stir until the sugar is dissolved. Add the juice and ice cubes and shake vigorously. Strain and serve.

Like Fernet Branca, Underberg is a form of bitters. Unlike Fernet Branca, the bottles do not itemize the ingredients, saying only 'made of a selection of the finest herbs from forty-three countries'. Underberg comes in little individual splits (two thirds of an ounce) and is highly alcoholic (84° proof).

The big difference between Fernet Branca and Underberg lies in the taste. FB is bitter, as bitters should be; Underberg carries a sweet overtaste of liquorice.

Underberg

One wee bottle, drunk neat

This simple remedy was popular in the good old days of the British Empire when far-flung officers' clubs were a place to unwind after a work-out with the Bengal Lancers and other troops.

British Empire*

a glass of warm soda water
5 drops of bitters

Mix and drink.

Ever wondered why you are thirsty the morning after? Well, there are two reasons, although most people don't realize it. Alcohol is not only a dehydrating agent. it is a diuretic as well! This means, in lay terms, that in addition to

*It is interesting to note that 'bitters and water' is also an old Irish remedy.

pulling the body juices from your system, it is making you urinate much more than you should. The whole body machine is being drained. This remedy, therefore, is important, and should always be used in addition to whatever other set of cures are appealing.

Liquids

water, ginger ale, soda, etc.

Take copiously.

NUTRITIONAL

This remedy is especially recommended for a small group of people who are all suffering.

Gail's Giggle

1 In a wok heat three tablespoonfuls of safflower oil, one tablespoonful of sesame oil.

2 Add two heads of broccoli, chopped and with bigger stems

49

removed. Add pepper, crushed red pepper and a thumb-sized piece of fresh ginger, grated. Stir-fry for two minutes until the vegetable is *al dente*. Remove from heat and add three teaspoonfuls of soy sauce. Mix.

Eat with fingers directly from wok, accompanied by a good imported beer.

This dish is rated highly for several reasons:

1 The vitamins in the broccoli.

2 The piquancy of taste in the mouth. (You should have added enough of the spices to achieve this.)

3 The pleasant clean sensation of eating crunchy salty food.

4 The convivial spirit of the communal eat.

5 The liquid, vitamins and alcoholic content of the beer.

This is not a recipe, it is a meal. Try it if you like, but unless you have the German penchant for heavy meals this may seem a bit onerous when all you want is to feel well again.

Katerfrühstück (Hangover breakfast)
herring with dill and sour cream garnish
sausages
ham
goulash soup
a stein of beer

Here is part of the Katerfrühstück that makes sense to eat. (Fish is used the world over for a hangover cure.) Do not plan, however, to toss this together the morning after.

Rollmopse (Herring rolls)

12 salt herring fillets
1/2 pint cider vinegar
1/2 pint cold water
3 juniper berries, 2 whole allspice, 3 cloves
6 crushed peppercorns
1 small bay leaf
1 1/2 tablespoonfuls German-style mustard
2 tablespoonfuls capers, drained
3 onions, peeled, sliced, separated into rings
2 large dill pickles, cut in wedges
parsley sprigs

Five or six days before:
1 Soak the herring fillets in water to cover for twelve hours in refrigerator, changing the water twice. Drain well, rinse under cold water; pat dry with paper towels and discard any bones.
2 Add the vinegar, water, juniper, allspice, cloves, peppercorns and bay leaf to two-quart saucepan and bring to boil over high heat. Reduce heat; simmer for five minutes; cool to room temperature.
3 Lay the herring fillets, skin side down, on tray. Spread one teaspoon of mustard on each fillet and scatter half a teaspoon of capers and several onion rings over the mustard. Place one pickle wedge at the narrow end of each fillet, and roll them swissroll fashion around the pickle. Skewer the rolls with toothpicks. Pack close together in a glass dish in two layers with remaining onion rings scattered between layers and on top. Pour the marinade over the herrings, then cover the dish and refrigerate.

Five mornings later:
1 Bring rollmopse to room temperature. Drain slightly, reserving the onion rings.
2 Arrange on platter and garnish with parsley.

Bartenders spend a good part of their early opening hours dishing out Bloody Marys and other hangover antidotes. Some of them, however, have their own formulae that they take when *they* have a hangover. Here is one from the man who pours at Daley's Dandelion, on the East Side of New York.

Bob Venezia

Place in a shaker:
2 eggs
2 teaspoonfuls sugar
2 teaspoonfuls vanilla yogurt
a little thick cream

Shake and drink.

Walter Matthau

ice cream

'I was drunk once – it was 1943 in Kearney, Nebraska. I tried ice cream to get over the hangover but that didn't work so I just suffered until the ice cream would stay down.'

The following is really nothing more than a very lumpy Virgin Mary, and comes from Peter Kreindler, *el jefe* of '21' in New York City.

Hangover Tomatoes

whole fresh tomatoes
Worcestershire sauce
tabasco

celery sticks, finely chopped
freshly ground pepper

Mash the mixture up until you have reduced it to small lumps. If the tomatoes are dry, add some tomato juice. Ladle into glasses.

Here is a recipe from the Middle Ages that is not worthy of notice except in that it reconfirms the long-time use of fish to deal with hangovers.

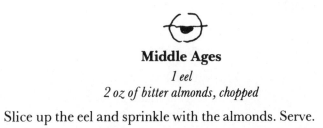

Middle Ages

1 eel
2 oz of bitter almonds, chopped

Slice up the eel and sprinkle with the almonds. Serve.

This cure precedes the following contemporary remedy by several hundred years, and may be considered obsolete as well as unfair.

Warau Indian
(for women only)

Take your mate when you come upon him the worse for wear and tie him, mummy-like, in a hammock until the siege is over.

This is the contemporary (and far more suitable) solution for a hangover south of the border. It was reported by Roger Simon of the *New York Post* as being unearthed by a *Time* correspondent, Roberto Suro.

Tratamiento de Choque
raw fish
lemon juice
onions
salsa picante (hot sauce)

Marinate the fish for two days in the lemon juice and onions. Add the hot sauce. Serve with popcorn and beer.

Here is a fabled cure, in both senses of the word – well known and not true. Caffeine may help keep you awake, or may get you awake, but it cannot eliminate the discomforts of a hangover.

Coffee
Strong, weak, American, European, black, with cream, sweetened, or not, perked, boiled or filtered.

The Plinys, like many other top-drawer Roman families, enjoyed the pleasures of good food and drink. Fortunately, they could also pen a word or two on the subject so that we are left with a little knowledge of their tastes.

Pliny the Elder, for example, was something of a cheese buff and was particularly attracted to pecorino – and not just any old pecorino, but the one made in Tuscany. And as wine goes so well with cheese it is not surprising that every now and then he overdid it. When that happened, the Pliny family knew just what to do.

Pliny the Elder

2 owl's eggs, raw

To be taken neat.

Devilish Eggs

1 clove of garlic, crushed
1 teaspoonful curry powder
1 teaspoonful butter
1 teaspoonful Bengal Club chutney (or, if unavailable, a different brand, finely chopped)
2 tablespoonfuls sour cream
1 teaspoonful chopped peanuts
4 hardboiled eggs

Cook the garlic and curry very gently in the butter for three minutes. Combine with the egg yolks and chutney and mix well; bind with sour cream. Fill into the egg halves and garnish with chopped peanuts. (Or eat the peanuts while you're getting the eggs ready.)

Bartenders see 'em come and see 'em go. Laughter, tears, fights, kisses, rich men, poor men, happy drinkers, drunks and alcoholics. Zay Smith, a bartender, according to Roger Simon, reports:

'People would come into the tavern in very bad shape and ask me for something to stop the pain ... Actually, this is not a cure for hangovers. It is a cure for hiccups. But these guys were so drunk, they didn't know the difference anyway.'

Zay Smith

Worcestershire sauce on a lemon wedge

You just close your eyes and bite the lemon wedge. It helps if you are standing up while you are doing this.

'I'd ask them if they felt better and they'd say, "Huh? Where am I?" So I guess it works.'

56

That.. better. be better..!

The logic of this cure is obvious from the discussion of the need to break down the congeners and aldehydes coursing through the bloodstream.

Fructose Fixer

oranges or lemons
honey

Squeeze the oranges or lemons or a mixture of the two. Add honey to taste, at least several tablespoons.

The Romans, of course, moved from orgy to orgy. Thus, they were in frequent need of something to pull them out of a hangover. They had a number of quite special remedies for this, such as a small plate of owlets' eyes. (Is this cure significantly related to the Pliny family cure, or is it only coincidence that owl parts exist in both?) As owlet eyes are nowadays quite hard to come by a second favourite Roman remedy is herewith presented: sheep lungs – known as *lights* among the cognoscenti. They can be prepared in any number of ways. The following version is taken from a mountain shepherd of Crete and can be adapted to suburban, if not urban, use.

Skewered Sheep Lights (Kokkoretsi)
1 sheep

Insert a knife into the throat of the sheep and rip down and outward, cutting the aorta and other arteries in one swift stroke. As soon as the animal is dead, skin it and gut it in the normal way. Now pull away, in a long swinging motion, the small intestines from the membrane that holds them. With the fingers of one hand strip their contents out as you amass the yardage. With the other hand gather the intestine in a coil, much like you would do with a hank of rope. Take a foot-long section of the *large* intestines (your casing) and stuff with chunks of the lungs. Cover this with the filigree fat that

58

covers the lower stomach of the beast. Next thread this crude sausage on to a skewer. Now take the small intestine that you have coiled and wrap it round and round the skewered meat, swaddling it, so to speak. Bind it tightly (you do not need to worry about tearing it: sheep intestine is strong stuff and is considered the finest quality surgical gut).

Place your skewer over a bed of coals – not so near that the dripping fat ignites and scorches the *kokkoretsi*. It is done in about twenty minutes, when the wrapping is nicely char-broiled.

Note: the proper herder's accompaniment to this dish would be a taste of *raki*, a fiery distillation of grape. Depending on whether you also wish a hair of the dog, you may want to follow this tradition or not.

This soup is filled with the right kinds of nutrients.

Clamato Broth

8 oz tomato juice
8 oz clam juice
juice of one lemon
a few leaves of fresh basil, if available
salt
pepper

Mix the ingredients in a saucepan, heat and serve. If you wish, you may add a dollop of sour cream to your soup bowl.

Tahiti.

You are lying in a nipa hut upon soft fronds, regretting having had quite so many coconut shells full of rum the night before. Presently a soft rustle makes you turn your head. A young fawn-coloured girl has entered the hut. She bends over you and wipes your forehead with a cold, wet cloth. A lei of jasmine falls away from her soft small breasts, and the smell of flowers fills your head. From behind her ear she removes a sprig of gardenia flowers and places it behind yours. Then, next to your bed she places a bowl and motions for you to eat. You can hardly take your eyes away from her delicate, supple body just inches from you. She smiles and, almost unconsciously, slightly quivers in her loins. The grass skirt shimmers and her flat stomach takes on the texture of gooseflesh. She touches you lightly on the lips and then points again to the bowl. You continue to lie motionless. Then she reaches over and takes a sliver of raw fish from the bowl and places it in your mouth . . .*

Pagoa

slices of raw tuna
juice of four lemons
one tomato, chopped
one clove garlic, one cucumber, and a pimento, all chopped

Mix all ingredients and allow to stand in a cool place for several hours before serving.

---

*This same dish, taken instead at a luncheon counter, rates only

Fish Fingers

1 can anchovy fillets, mashed
1 onion, sliced paper-thin
3 slices pumpernickel bread
black pepper
olive oil

Cut each slice of bread into three strips; spread the anchovy paste on these. Cover with onion slices, brush with olive oil, dust with pepper. Heat briefly under a grill until the onions start to change colour.

Although this book has not quoted them often, there are many people – especially inhabitants of the soft underbelly of Europe – who insist that a mug of hot chicken soup is just the thing the morning after. Perhaps. But in any case, it is a nice drink after a day of skiing, splitting wood, and other outdoor labours.

This dish, like many simple peasant recipes, is best made a day ahead, then reheated. (Therefore, if it is to be a cure for the hangover, there must be thought afore malice.)

Chicken Soup

1 old chicken, or chicken carcass
2 onions, sliced
2 carrots, sliced
greens (lettuce, watercress, parsley, etc.)
peppercorns, salt
2 cloves of garlic, mashed
tarragon

Put all the ingredients except the tarragon in a saucepan with two quarts of water. (If the chicken leftovers included stuf-

61

fing, add that also.) Cook, covered, until the liquid is reduced by almost half. Strain. Just before serving add a half-teaspoon of tarragon (and a splash of cream, if desired).

Here is another soup that has its fans. Like the chicken soup it also works well as an equalizer for a good day's work. The beets and cabbage are, of course, rich in the right kind of vitamins to trump a hangover. There are many recipes for borscht. This one is medium-easy and very good.

Borscht
1 lb cubed lean beef and a marrow bone
1 clove garlic
1 each carrot, celery, leek, bay leaf
12 peppercorns
6 beets
¼ cabbage, shredded
bunch of fresh dill
sour cream
salt

Cook the beef, garlic, carrots, celery, leek, bayleaf and peppercorns gently in two quarts of water, covered, for two hours. Meanwhile cook the unpeeled beets in a separate saucepan until soft. Peel and dice. Strain the beef soup and add the beets and shredded cabbage. Cook another twenty minutes. Add salt to taste. Serve in bowls with minced dill on top and a tablespoon of sour cream in each.

Cabbage appears in the hangover cures of many cultures and, like the similar deployment of fish for the purpose, proves that great drinking minds think alike. In Alsace and other kraut-prone areas they will banish a hangover by swilling the juice of sauerkraut. In Yugoslavia they allow the cabbage to pickle until the exudate runs red and imbibe that to the same effect. The Egyptians chewed boiled cabbage to get rid of hangovers. The ancients of Rome, too, used to rely on cabbage, but the relationship between cabbage and spirits is even older.

As Waverly Root notes: 'Dionysus, the god of wine, caught Lycurgus, king of the Thracian Edonians, in the sacrilegious act of pulling up grapevines. He tied him to a grape stalk to await punishment, the anticipation of which caused Lycurgus to weep profusely, and with reason, for he was subsequently blinded and then torn limb from limb. Where his tears fell the first cabbages sprang up.'

While anyone who wishes can press the juice out of some sauerkraut and drink it, a more flavourful rendering of the magic plant follows in a good soup recipe. (This soup is best made the night before, or even earlier and frozen for emergency use.)

Cabbage Soup

Follow the recipe for borscht, eliminating the beets, doubling the amount of cabbage, adding two pinches of caraway seeds and half a pint of cider.

Many hangover remedies have exotic names, e.g. Moose Milk, Bloody Mary, which of course are only metaphoric. Not so this one.

This recipe is for the bird owner who awakes tormented by the sound of chirping in the cage across the room. It provides only modest nutrition.

Fried Canary

1 canary
1 pint cooking oil
salt and pepper to taste

Grab the canary and with a large pair of scissors cut off its head. Make a small incision in the skin near the breast-bone; slip a finger inside, and deftly pull off the skin with all the feathers attached. Heat the oil until almost smoking, pop the bird in, undrawn, and deep-fry for two minutes. Remove from the oil, dust with salt and pepper and serve. (Some people recommend flambéing the canary with cognac immediately upon removing from the pan. This step is optional.)

Here is another nutritious soup, only this one, being cold, is best for summertime. There are an infinite number of variations in the preparation of this soup, so feel free to modify as much as you wish. Do not skimp on the tomatoes, however, as they are the richest source of potassium and vitamin C.

Gazpacho

1 1/2 lb tomatoes
1 cucumber
2 spring onions
1 green pepper
3 tablespoonfuls olive oil
1 clove garlic
1 small bunch of parsley
salt, pepper, cayenne to taste

Chop all the vegetables very thin, add the olive oil and seasonings. Allow to stand for twelve hours. Add cold water or tomato juice to bring the mixture to a proper consistency. Serve.

No discussion of the pleasures and pains of drink would be complete without mention of Samuel Pepys. This renowned journalist, perhaps most famous for his oft-used line, 'and so to bed', was always going on and off the wagon.*

'Thanks be to God since my leaving drinking of wine, I do find myself much better, and do mind my business better and do spend less money, and less time lost in idle company.'

And: 'At last, our business being most spent we went into Mrs Mercer's and there mighty merry, smutting one another with candle grease and soot, till most of us were like devils. And that being done, then we broke up and to my house; and there I made them drink, and upstairs we went

---

*The term 'on the wagon', meaning off liquor, comes from an earlier expression: 'I've gone on the water wagon'.

and then fell into dancing ... and mighty mirth we had, and Mercer danced a jigg; and Nan Wright and my wife and Pegg Pen put on perriwigs. Thus we spent till three or four in the morning, mighty merry ...'

Pepys had a number of hangover remedies, including drinking whey, horseradish ale and turpentine. As the former two are not easily available and the latter somewhat chancy, we select the following from his suggestions.

Samuel Pepys
One quart of orange juice, laced with sugar

HAIR OF THE DOG

The majority of hangover cures throughout history right up into contemporary times have included a certain amount of alcoholic spirits in the formula. This predilection is based on sound medical logic. There is, however, a distinction – albeit minor – between those potions created especially to serve a predetermined medical need and the alcohol-based cures which were constructed from instinct rather than from methodology.

For over four centuries the latter group has been known by the rubric 'hair of the dog', a phrase first noted by John Heywood in 1546. Heywood wrote:

I pray thee let me and my fellow have
A Haire of the dog that bit us last night.

The aphorism has stood the test of time* and has only recently been challenged. Thomas Abercrombie has

---

* *Cf* Ben Jonson: ''Twas a hot night with some of us last night, John: shall we pluck a hair of the same wolf today, proctor John?'

suggested that the phrase be changed to 'hair*s* of the dog', and Cyril Connolly that the word 'hair' be replaced by 'tuft'. I am inclined to agree. The image is more zesty, assertive – even if more hairy.

The verity that 'hair of the dog' cures are effective was given a boost by one Dr James L. Hoon not long ago. According to news reports, the good doctor 'photographed the turbulent stomach activity of two persons suffering from hangover'. (This he accomplished with the use of a miniature camera that he had manoeuvred down the subjects' throats into their tummies by means of a piece of flexible tubing.) 'Then he gave each victim an ounce and a half of liquor, waited for five minutes, and photographed their stomachs again. The second set of pictures showed that the liquor had a "remarkable calming" effect, Dr Hoon said.'

Of course it is possible that the mere placement of the photographic equipment into their innards worked as a placebo.

Basic Hair

One slug of alcohol (brand is optional).

There really is a drink with this name!

Hair of the dog cocktail
1 1/2 oz scotch
1 tablespoonful honey
1 tablespoonful double cream

Shake or blend briefly with ice. Strain and serve.

Eddie Condon
'Take the juice of two quarts of whisky . . .'

Ed McMahon, the voluble sideman on the *Tonight* show in America, offers a good basic formula for a cure that has many variations.

Ed McMahon

ice-cold beer*
4 jiggers of Angostura bitters

Mix and drink

Among the many things that the French culture has given us is a wonderful sense of expressiveness. Even their phrase for hangover, *gueule de bois*, has style. Instead of using the obvious word for mouth, *bouche*, they selected one normally used in describing the physiognomy of an animal. Hence it is 'snout of wood' instead of the far less interesting concept of 'mouth of wood'. Following their example, perhaps the whole experience of 'the morning after' should be recast in the nomenclature of a quadruped. Thus we would speak of aching withers, rasping lights, a bothersome cud, etc.

Another fine French expression is *rince l'oeil*, literally an 'eye rinse'. To a Frenchman an example might be groggily walking down a dreary street and glancing up to espy a seventeen-year-old girl admiring her naked body in a mirror. They also have a *rince cochon*, or pig rinse.

Rince Cochon

A small amount of lemon syrup in a wine glass. Fill halfway with dry white wine. Top with soda water.

---

*Others modify this by using flat and/or warm beer.

W. C. Fields, as noted earlier, left no ambiguity about his drinking preferences. When once asked if he wanted a chaser of water he replied, 'Watah – fish fuck in water!' His hangover cure:

W. C. Fields

a martini made of 1 part vermouth, 4 parts gin and one olive

To be taken around the clock.

Scott and Zelda Fitzgerald drank their way through two continents, terrifying some, disgusting others and thrilling even more. The Fitzgerald cure is found in a note which he wrote upon the request of a friend that he write something especially for her. He wrote (*sic*):

Skot Fisgurel
by Merry Mac-Caul

'I have never scene Skot Fisgurelsober but he is a grate freind of mine. He has offen toled me about his methods. He begins in the mawning with 3 (three) strong whiskeys and from then on for years and years he seldom stops. I myself am a danscer and kan skarecely write my own name.'*

Like the Bloody Mary, this drink has many variants of its ingredients. The basic one offered here comes from Elizabeth Taylor.

Bullshot
4 oz cold consommé, spiced with salt and pepper
juice of one lemon
dash of horseradish
'just enough' vodka
Serve in a glass over ice.

●

And here is another version from Toots Shor.

Bullshot II
4 oz cold consommé
2 teaspoonfuls Worcestershire sauce
2 teaspoonfuls ketchup
dash of pepper
2 dashes of vinegar
yolk of a raw egg
Drink in one gulp.

Is there any doubt about which recipe will be the one you choose?

---

*From *Exiles from Paradise: Zelda and Scott Fitzgerald* by Sara Mayfield, Delacorte Press, New York, 1976.

Dean Martin

'Stay Drunk.'

Rye whisky is no longer as fashionable a drink as it once was. It has been replaced by sour-mash bourbons, single-malt scotches and other epicurean drinks. But rye did have its day. Here are two hangover remedies featuring the whisky.

Morning Fizz

1 oz rye
2 oz Pernod
1 teaspoonful sugar
juice of half a lemon

●

Jimmy Glennon
(barkeep at P. J. Clarke's in New York)
a shot of rye with a little bitters in it

Julia Child, apart from being an inspiration in the preparation of regal dishes in the home kitchen, is also a pragmatist. She reports that she doesn't have 'time to be non-compos the next morning'. Ironically her husband's cure, which she says

'might make you a little happier if nothing else', is the most detailed and aromatic creation in this compendium and goes by the name of 'A la Recherche de l'Orange Perdue'.

Julia Child:

'Know your limits.'*

A la Recherche de l'Orange Perdue

___

* As Dorothy Parker once observed: 'One more drink and I'd be under the host.'

½ pint Meyers dark rum
4 tablespoonfuls Rose's lime juice
juice one fresh lime
4 tablespoonfuls orange curaçao
1 tablespoonful bitter orange marmalade
½ pint French white vermouth
1 whole orange cut into pieces, rind and all
5 drops orange bitters
6 ice cubes

Blend it all for twenty seconds and strain twice into a pitcher. This serves four people.

What distinguishes one hair of the dog from another is the logic of the ingredients. Here we find vodka (low in congeners), curaçao (of orange extract) and cream. All of these ingredients make sense following the discussion in Chapter 2.

White Shoulders

1 oz vodka
½ oz curaçao
1 oz double cream

Shake with ice, strain and serve.

This recipe comes from the indefatigable Kingsley Amis.

Polish Bison

1 generous teaspoonful Bovril (beef extract)
1 (adjustable) tot vodka
water
a squeeze of lemon juice (optional)
a shake of pepper

'Make the Bovril as if you were merely making Bovril and stir the other stuff in. Named in salute to the nation that makes the best vodka, but its product will be wasted in this mixture; use a British version. This is a very cheery concoction, especially in cold and/or hungover conditions.'

Moose Milk

4 tablespoonfuls vodka
1 egg
2 oz sugar
1 tablespoonful orange-flower water
4 tablespoonfuls lemon juice
6 ice cubes, cracked
³/4 pint milk

Add all the ingredients except the milk and blend at high speed for ten seconds. Add the milk and mix briefly. Makes two very large drinks.

This remedy has such a wonderful name that it demands inclusion even though there is nothing special about its properties to distinguish it from countless other cocktails that might serve as a hair of the dog.

Between the Sheets

¹/2 oz each Cointreau, light rum, brandy
1 teaspoonful lemon juice

Shake, strain and serve.

Nogs are a hair of the dog buffered by the other ingredients. You may or may not like the thought of swallowing a mixture of cream and raw eggs the morning after a heavy bout of drinking, but if you do, then a nog may be just the thing. It also carries a plethora of festive images.

Nog

1 egg
1 tablespoonful sugar
4 tablespoonfuls cream
4 tablespoonfuls liquor (rum, brandy, bourbon, etc.)
nutmeg

Mix the egg yolk, sugar and part of the liquor together. Allow to stand for at least an hour. (This gets rid of the eggy taste.) Add the rest of the liquor, fold in the egg white beaten stiff, dust with nutmeg and serve.

Whether it is the Cajun, Creole, French or jazz influence it is impossible to determine, but for some reason New Orleans is a town associated with nights of drinking and merriment. At some of the local (i.e. tourist) eateries it is almost assumed that in addition to a ration of Eggs Benedict* a customer is going to order a pick-me-up. Here is one from the place.

---

*Eggs Benedict, by the way, is a dish named after Lemuel Benedict, who was suffering from a hangover one morning in 1894 at the Waldorf Hotel in New York. He ordered food that he thought would get him rid of the problem: poached eggs on ham on buttered toast (now English muffin) with hollandaise sauce. The maître d'hôtel named the dish after him.

Sazerac

1 oz Pernod
1 oz whisky
1 teaspoonful sugar
1 dash bitters

Shake with ice, strain and serve with a lemon twist.

Back in the wonderful days of transatlantic steamers and white flannels a good evening of drink and witty talk was part of a 'crossing'. William Astor Chanler reports that one Harvard wag who was part of the Cunard set insisted that a Sherry Flip was the perfect preparation the following morning before a game of quoits.

Sherry Flip

2 oz sherry
1 teaspoonful sugar
1 egg
nutmeg

Place the first three contents in one of the old-fashioned cocktail shakers that you can *really* shake, add ice and shake like hell. Strain into a glass and dust with nutmeg.

The following cure, detailed by Waverley Root, is listed without a symbol of its efficiency coefficient. The reason for this is that none of this book's accredited evaluators were willing to drink the concoction. According to Mr Root, Las Vegas is credited with developing this very special mixture.

Las Vegas

¾ glass of tomato juice
2 tablespoonfuls cream
1 raw egg
pinch of nutmeg
3 oz beer

After combining the first four ingredients it 'would then seem ready to drink, but some power has decreed that three ounces of beer should be added to it'.

Here is a quite classic remedy that combines both an antacid with a hair of the dog. Its single failing is the call for golden tequila which, as Chapter 2 made obvious, is going to contain more congeners than the clear type. It is named after the man whose research uncovered the formula.

Thomas Abercrombie

2 Alka Seltzer tablets
1 double shot of José Cuervo Tequila Gold

Drop the tablets in the liquor, allow to fizz for four seconds, drink.

In the western United States 'prairie oysters' is slang for bulls' testicles which are fried up and eaten with gusto after the annual castration of cattle. That dish, however, has not yet been thoroughly tested for its efficacy in curing hangovers. The Prairie Oyster that follows derives its name from the egg yolk that peeks up from the glass at you. (In some bars the egg has now been replaced by an actual mollusc which, to reduce confusion, should probably be renamed the Prairie Bivalve.

Prairie Oyster

1 egg
1 tablespoonful Worcestershire sauce
1 1/2 oz port
celery salt
freshly ground black pepper

Slide the egg yolk into a four-ounce wine or cocktail glass without breaking the thing. Dust with the pepper, colour a little with the Worcestershire sauce. Then add the port. Sprinkle with the celery salt. Now try to swallow the affair without breaking the yolk.

In the good old days before World War II there were a number of international watering places at which the literati and other creative souls would linger. (It is not entirely irrelevant at this point to note that one reason artists are often heavy drinkers is not to stimulate the creative juices*, but merely because, unlike the rest of the working populace, they do no need to get up in the morning and go to the office or factory.) At any rate, a number of these hotels and affiliated bars became known for their special drinks which may, or may not, have cleared such heads as those of Hemingway, Fitzgerald, Maugham. The cures on the two following pages are from those earlier days.

The Suffering Bastard was introduced to the world by Shepheard's Hotel in Cairo and is herewith described according to James Beard.

---

* 'Possum nilego subrius' (Martial).

Suffering Bastard*

1/2 jigger of brandy
1/2 jigger of gin
1/2 jigger of Rose's lime juice
2 dashes bitters

'Pour into a tall glass with ice and add ginger ale and fresh mint. Just mix it up and you're on the road – whatever road that may be.'

Many authorities, including Waverley Root, ascribe the invention of the Bloody Mary to Harry's New York Bar in Paris. Another claimant, however, is the St Regis bar in New York and its tender Fernand Petiot. According to the *New York Post*, in the latter case the drink evolves first from a breakfast drink of John Jacob Astor, who built the place. Some years after J.A. went down on the *Titanic*, Petiot took the Astor mix of vodka and tomato juice and spiced it up with a little Worcestershire sauce. This drink he named the Red

*Also sometimes spelled as the Suffern Bawstard.

Snapper, which eventually became the Bloody Mary.

Today there are numerous recipes for the drink. Some include celery, some not; certain cognoscenti say only a wedge of *lemon* may be used, while others use lime. In any case, here is the version of '21', a place people consider classy, and a place that serves *a lot* of drinks.

Bloody Mary

1 1/2 oz vodka, chilled
2 oz tomato juice, chilled
dash Worcestershire sauce
salt, celery salt, black pepper, to taste
tabasco (optional)

Shake well and pour into a chilled cocktail glass.

Raffles was one of the great 'old world' hotels, which when the author visited it in 1964 appeared unchanged in its spacious, shaded rooms with cooling overhead fans, and large verandas. Raffles is the first home of the Singapore Sling

Singapore Sling

1/2 oz Cherry Heering
1/2 oz lemon juice
3 fl oz gin
ice
water

Pour first three ingredients into a glass over ice, mix and top with water. Stir and enjoy.

Out in the desert one might expect a hangover remedy to be some sort of thirst quencher. The following concoction, however, comes from Ely, Nevada, and is named for the lady who makes it in the Ely Hotel (which was *not* a watering place of Maugham, *et alii*).

Marianne

¹/₂ oz Fernet Branca
¹/₂ oz whisky

Mix and belt it down.

●

Not everyone in Ely agrees with Marianne, however. One resident of the town and a patron of Marianne's bar insists that the following is a more effective cure. (One can surmise from the recipe that the gentleman is of either Yugoslavian or Alsacian heritage.)

Chez Marianne I

3 oz saurkraut juice
¹/₂ oz olive oil
pepper

Drink 'reel' fast, then eat smoked bacon.

●

And a waitress at Marianne's place has yet another remedy, proving that Ely, Nevada, is a place of considerable creativity.

Chez Marianne II

ice-cold orange juice
2 raw eggs

Stir and drink

To understand the effectiveness of this old standby, remember (1) vitamins in beer (stout is vitamin-rich beer) and (2) the role of effervescence in accelerating the effect of alcohol.

It will become immediately obvious that the Black Velvet is a twofer.

Black Velvet

cold champagne
cold stout (Guinness is traditional)

Place a tall chilled glass before you, and with a bottle of the above in each hand pour equally until the glass is full.

Rasputin may have been mad but he was no dummie. Clams and olives are loaded with the right vitamins, and vodka is the perfect hair accompaniment. We cannot be sure that the remedy comes from the lips of the mighty Russian himself or if it was just named for his eminence. Research on whether anchovy-stuffed olives were available in nineteenth-century Russia would, of course, settle the matter . . .

Rasputin

1 1/2 oz vodka
3 oz clam juice
one anchovy-stuffed olive

Mix and serve in a very large Martini glass.

P. J. Clarke's is a very famous New York bar. It was also the location for the filming of *The Lost Weekend*. According to Charlie Clarke, nephew of the original P. J., Ray Milland's favourite pick-me-up during the filming was a Shandygaff.

Shandygaff

Pour into a glass equal amounts of ginger beer and beer

MISCELLANEOUS

You don't see many people walking around sporting garlands and wreaths very much any more, but it used to be considered a nifty way to prevent and cure a hangover. Here are just a couple of examples.

Ancient Greece
a garland of parsley

Worn the night before to ward off a hangover.

●

Ancient Rome
a garland of celery

Also worn the night before for the same reason.

Anthony Haden-Guest, who chronicles the comings and goings of New York's cultural and social movers, suggests this interesting mixture.

Anthony Haden-Guest
Buck's Fizz
(half champagne, half orange juice)
&
an art gallery*

---

* 'There's nothing so calming to the head as the Dutch School. No wonder so many Vermeers have been stolen.'

This is certainly the most passive set of prescriptions for dealing with a hangover. All of these remedies fall under the *endure it* category, and many would say were quite unbecoming to a twentieth-century entrepreneur.

Sleep, Quiet, Darkness and Time

Ash Wednesday

In keeping with the spirit of Lenten abstinence, smash all the bottles in the house and fast for forty days. If you are still alive at the end of this time you will nonetheless be much too sick to be messing with alcohol again.

Anyone who saw the movie *Marathon Man* will remember the gruesome scene in which Laurence Olivier drills a couple of Dustin Hoffman's teeth full of holes in order to learn how much he knows. They will also probably remember the doctor's remedy for ending the excruciating pain: wiping on a bit of oil of cloves. Thus this cure, which was popular in ancient times, makes sense on the surface of it. Nonetheless, one cannot help but wonder this: if a dab of clove oil can anaesthetize drilled tooth nerves, might not a broth of the same be a bit extreme for the mundane hangover?

Ancient Times

handful of cloves
water

Make a broth of cloves by boiling them in water for a while. Drink and be merry.

Back at the '21' bar at closing time one rainy night during the war, Robert Benchley asked the uniformed man at the door to call him a cab, whereupon the man drew himself up to full height and said, 'Sir, I am an Admiral of the United States Navy.' Benchley quickly replied, 'Good, call me a boat.'*

This man, who brought us wonderful times of laughter, by his extreme prescription below provides a *bona fide* cure, not because it must be understood as literal but because its humorous hyperbole can bring a smile to the spirit.

Robert Benchley

'There is no cure for the hangover, save death.'

---

*From *21 – The Life and Times of New York's Favourite Club*, by Marilyn Kaytor, Viking Press, 1975.

For the insecure, the oversensitive, the masochistic, the show-off type, the teetotaller, the man about-to-lose-his-job-if-he-is-late-again or the man who cannot afford the luxury of drink, this is a wonderful and inexpensive cure.

Guilt

Any expression of this can do – from the simple hanging one's head low and begging a spouse's forgiveness, to assertively smashing a brick wall with the bare fists until the knuckles are bleeding (modest guilt) or crushed (extreme guilt).

The Romans, as noted elsewhere, could 'party' for days on end. Some historians even suggest that this behaviour was terminal for their empire, which seems a bit extreme especially as they knew how to avoid morning-after effects. Understanding that the body needs a periodic cleansing they would repair during an orgy to an antechamber (called in Latin a *vomitorium*) and with the aid of a feather tickle up from the stomach all the substances from which the thrill had gone. Then back to the party.

Roman

1 small room
1 feather (ostrich or other large plumed bird)
(optional) 1 slave to hold the bowl

Do like the Romans.

It is curious that quite particular remedies sometimes pop up independently in two distant locations. Two examples follow.

Some of the residents of 700 Acre Island, a small spa in the Maine archipelago, elect an early morning plunge in the ocean (water temperature 50°F) for hangovers in summertime; but in winter the sea is frozen, so they do the next best thing. This is paralleled by the suggestion of H. Allen Smith reported recently in the *Washington Post*.

700 Acre Island
Roll naked in the snow until you can't stand it anymore.

●

H. Allen Smith
'Lie face down in a snow drift.'

The following cure has been noted in such diverse places as among the US Armed Services operating in West Germany and lobstermen along the Maine coast near Lincolnville.

Flat Beer

Open a bottle the night before. Drink when flat in the a.m.

If you have a lot of time and a small cedar house with a powerful heater, by all means take a sauna. This Nordic speciality has also been used in similar forms among many cultures, e.g. the North American Indian sweat lodges. Saunas and the like cause heavy sweating, which opens the pores and rids the system of waste minerals. A sauna also speeds the metabolism, but as an extra fillip try the Finnish trick of beating yourself – or your partner – with birch switches. This definitely gets the blood racing. You will probably want to stop short of the Greek variant for hangovers which called for out-and-out flagellation.

Saunas

After checking with your doctor to ensure that a sauna is safe for you, heat to at least 200°F. Enter and sweat. (Whipping is optional.) If you are fortunate, upon exiting, to find snow, complete the programme with the 700 Acre Island remedy (see page 90).

This is definitely the cure for families on a low budget, but unfortunately it is not all that effective. Water will quench a parched throat, wet the dry mouth and begin to restore a proper liquid balance to the body. It can do nothing, however, for dilated blood vessels, nor eradicate congeners, fusel oils, unmetabolized alcohol still in the system, etc.

Water

Drink at will. To add a little flourish, call it by it's synonym, Adam's Ale.

In the entire research field of hangovers Kingsley Amis stands supreme. Not only has he perceptively divided hangovers into physical and metaphysical afflictions, but he has also plumbed deeply the less humdrum cures. Some of his crafty suggestions include: shaving, reading from *Paradise Lost*, going up in an open-air plane, going down into a mine with the early morning shift to pick away at the coal-face.

The Amis cure below is distinguished by the fact that it copes with both physical and metaphysical hangovers simultaneously.

Kingsley Amis

Upon awakening: 'If your wife or other partner is beside you, and (of course) is willing, perform the sexual act as vigorously as you can. The exercise will do you good, and – on the assumption that you enjoy sex – you will feel toned up emotionally.

'*Warnings:* (1) if you are in bed with somebody you should not be in bed with, and have *in the least degree* a bad conscience about this, abstain. Guilt and shame are prominent constituents of the Metaphysical Hangover, and will certainly be sharpened by indulgence on such an occasion.

'(2) For the same generic reason, do not take the matter into your own hands if you awake by yourself.'

> Sometimes I think I'm nothing more to you than a hangover cure!

Robin Hollis, director of marketing for Maxwell's Plum, a watering place that causes (and cures) a lot of hangovers every day, offers two unrelated suggestions.

Robin Hollis I

Make a drink of half tomato juice and half beer (a Red Eye). It has the advantage of both coating your stomach and giving a small hair of the dog.

●

Robin Hollis II

Eat some Carr's Water Biscuits. It will help dry up the alcohol and take the filthy taste out of your mouth.

One might be tempted to discount this ancient Assyrian remedy were it not for two corroborating pieces of evidence. The first comes from Rome: in addition to owlet eyes and sheep lights they were partial to a spoonful of swallow-beak ashes. The second comes from none other than the brothers Branca, who in their bitters include myrrh among the ingredients.

Assyrian Paste

1 teaspoonful ground swallow's beak
1 teaspoonful myrrh

Mix together and eat. Follow with a glass of water if necessary.

Lord Byron had, of course, Milton's *oeuvre* available to him, but chose his own cure rather than preempt Kingsley Amis's recent canny usage. However, Byron may have had trouble with Milton's poetry. As a character Rutley pointed out, in a play of the same name, the only verse more deadly than Milton's Latin poetry was his English poetry.

Lord Byron

'Let us have wine and women, mirth and laughter, Sermons and soda-water the day after.'

You may laugh this one off if you dare; but beware! It is possible someone will start putting pins into a little doll that looks very much like you.

Haitian Voodoo

Stick thirteen pins into the cork of the bottle from which you were drinking.

Another remedy that is based in some sense on faith comes from Puerto Rico. It is not entirely coincidental, one would imagine, that Waverley Root concludes a long article on hangovers with this very suggestion. And we, too.

Puerto Rican Faith Healer
Take half a lemon and rub it in the armpits.